AF426360

Genesis Redefined

BRIDGING EVOLUTION AND DIVINITY

Author:

RAMESHWAR RAJ VOGGU

Genesis Redefined

CONTENTS

INTRODUCTION

In our childhood, many of us grew up learning the story of Adam and Eve, the first humans according to the Bible, and were taught that we are their descendants. But does this make sense when we look at the evidence provided by science and ancient beliefs? "Genesis Redefined: Bridging Evolution and Divinity" aims to shed light on this question and challenge the conventional narrative of human origins.

The story of Adam and Eve has long been embedded in our cultural consciousness, painting a picture of the beginning of humanity. Yet, as our understanding of science deepens, particularly through the theory of evolution proposed by Charles Darwin, the simplicity of this tale begins to show its limitations. At the same time, ancient philosophies like Hinduism offer a rich tapestry of wisdom that speaks to the nature of creation, life, and the cosmos.

This book seeks to bridge the gap between these two worlds—science and spirituality—to present a unified vision of our origins. It invites readers to reconsider long-held beliefs and open their minds to a perspective that marries the insights of evolutionary biology with the timeless knowledge found in Hindu teachings.

 By combining Darwin's groundbreaking theories with the spiritual principles of Hinduism, we can uncover a more nuanced and interconnected story of how life began and how divinity and evolution might not be at odds but are part of a greater cosmic dance.

So, let us embark on a journey of exploration and discovery. Let us question the familiar, challenge the conventional, and reimagine our understanding of where we come from.

- Rameshwar Raj

ABOUT THE AUTHOR

Rameshwar Raj
Founder - RAM&CO

Hi, I'm Rameshwar Raj, the founder of RAM&CO Group and the author of Genesis Redefined. Through this book, I aim to guide you on an extraordinary journey that challenges traditional beliefs and connects the dots between evolution and spirituality. My goal is to provide clarity, spark curiosity, and inspire a deeper understanding of our origins by blending science and ancient wisdom.

CHAPTER - 1
THE ADAM AND EVE

CHAPTER - 1
THE ADAM AND EVE

We all know the biblical story of Adam and Eve, the supposed first humans created by God. According to the Bible, God formed Adam from dust and breathed life into him. Later, to provide him companionship, Eve was created from one of Adam's ribs. They lived in the paradise of the Garden of Eden, innocent and pure, until they disobeyed God by eating the forbidden fruit, which introduced sin and mortality into the world.

This story has been passed down for generations, forming a core belief for many about the origin of humanity. It portrays a divine creation narrative filled with symbolism, moral teachings, and spiritual significance. But when we step into the realm of science and explore the evidence laid out by evolutionary biology, anthropology, and genetics, the story takes a fascinating turn.

Does it make sense in today's age of scientific advancement to believe that all humans descended solely from Adam and Eve? Can this traditional narrative align with the findings of Darwinian evolution or the discoveries of modern science? While faith and religious beliefs are deeply respected, this book seeks to examine these ancient stories in light of science, without undermining their cultural and spiritual significance.

Here, we will explore the contrast between religious myths and scientific evidence. This chapter serves as a stepping stone into a larger conversation, questioning the literal interpretation of Adam and Eve while connecting it to evolutionary biology. Prepare to dive deep into thought-provoking ideas as we bridge the gap between what we've been told and what science reveals.

CHAPTER - 2
About the Evolution

CHAPTER - 2
About the Evolution

Evolution is one of the most fascinating and revolutionary concepts in science. It explains how living organisms develop and diversify from earlier forms over millions of years. First proposed by Charles Darwin in his groundbreaking work On the Origin of Species, the theory of evolution fundamentally transformed our understanding of life on Earth. But how did life begin, and what is the path that led from simple organisms to complex beings like humans?

1. The Origin of Life: From Simple to Complex

The story of life's beginnings begins in the primordial oceans of Earth. About 3.5 to 4 billion years ago, the Earth was a molten mass with an atmosphere composed mainly of gases like methane, ammonia, and hydrogen. Over time, as the planet cooled, these conditions allowed for the formation of basic chemical compounds. Scientists believe that life originated through a process called abiogenesis, where simple organic molecules formed spontaneously in a water-rich environment.

The famous Miller-Urey experiment in 1953 demonstrated that amino acids—building blocks of proteins—could be synthesized in a lab under conditions that mimicked early Earth's atmosphere. This experiment gave rise to the hypothesis that life may have originated from a primordial soup, where chemical reactions eventually led to the creation of the first simple, self-replicating molecules. These molecules evolved over millions of years into more complex structures.

2. The First Forms of Life: Single-Celled Organisms

The earliest life forms were simple, single-celled organisms known as prokaryotes. These cells were the ancestors of modern bacteria and archaea. These primitive organisms were the first to harness energy through processes like photosynthesis and chemosynthesis, which gradually changed the Earth's atmosphere. For billions of years, these organisms ruled the planet, thriving in diverse environments, from deep ocean vents to the surface waters.

One significant evolutionary milestone was the development of eukaryotic cells, which are more complex and contain a nucleus. These cells evolved from prokaryotic ancestors and gave rise to more complex life forms. Eukaryotic cells enabled the development of multicellular organisms, a crucial step in the evolution of complex life.

3. The Transition from Water to Land

Approximately 500 million years ago, life began to adapt to life outside water. Early aquatic organisms faced the challenge of surviving in a new environment, leading to the evolution of structures that could support life on land. One of the earliest adaptations was the development of limbs and lungs, enabling fish-like organisms to crawl onto land and breathe air. These organisms evolved into amphibians, the first vertebrates to live both in water and on land.

Amphibians eventually gave rise to reptiles, which were better adapted for terrestrial life due to their tough, waterproof skin and the ability to lay eggs with hard shells. This adaptation helped them thrive in dry environments and marked a significant evolutionary step that set the stage for the development of more complex land-dwelling animals.

4. The Rise of Mammals and Early Ancestors of Humans

About 300 million years ago, reptiles ruled the land, but their reign was disrupted by a mass extinction event about 66 million years ago, possibly caused by an asteroid impact. This extinction paved the way for mammals to rise and dominate the Earth. Mammals were warm-blooded, had hair, and gave birth to live young, making them more adaptable to different climates and conditions.

Among these mammals were primates, the group of animals that eventually gave rise to humans. Primates evolved traits such as opposable thumbs, which allowed for greater dexterity, and larger brains relative to body size. Over millions of years, primates evolved into various species, leading to the development of hominids—early human-like creatures.

5. The Journey from Apes to Early Humans

Hominids began to show more human-like traits about 7 million years ago, with Sahelanthropus tchadensis being one of the earliest known hominids. These early ancestors were still adapted to both arboreal (tree-dwelling) and terrestrial life but started showing signs of bipedalism, walking on two legs.

As time went on, hominids evolved into different species, including Australopithecus afarensis, known for the famous fossil "Lucy." This species had a smaller brain size compared to modern humans but displayed clear evidence of bipedalism. The development of bipedal walking was crucial as it freed the hands for tool use and carrying objects.

The genus Homo emerged around 2.5 million years ago, with Homo habilis being one of the first members. Homo habilis had a larger brain than its predecessors and is believed to have used basic stone tools. Over time, Homo erectus appeared, with a more advanced toolset and the ability to use fire. They spread out of Africa and into Europe and Asia, showcasing an adaptability that led to the survival of the species.

6. The Evolution of Modern Humans

Homo sapiens, the species to which we belong, first appeared around 300,000 years ago in Africa. Unlike earlier hominids, modern humans developed advanced cognitive abilities, including complex language, abstract thinking, and the capacity for art and culture. These traits enabled the development of sophisticated societies, trade, and the ability to manipulate the environment in ways that no other species could.

As humans continued to evolve, they coexisted with other hominids, such as the Neanderthals and Denisovans, who had distinct traits and cultures. Genetic evidence suggests that there was interbreeding between Homo sapiens and these other hominids, which influenced the genetic makeup of modern humans.

7. Evolution's Ultimate Lesson: The Interconnection of Life

Evolution is a testament to the interconnectedness of all living things. From the simplest single-celled organisms in the primordial soup to the diverse and complex species we see today, the process of evolution has shaped life as we know it. The story of evolution is not just the story of survival; it is a story of adaptation, resilience, and continuous change.

As we move forward, this chapter sets the stage for exploring how these evolutionary insights align with ancient beliefs and the concept of divine purpose. How can the complex process of evolution coexist with the idea of a creator? Is there room for both science and spirituality in explaining human origins? This is the bridge we seek to cross, as we delve deeper into understanding evolution's role in the grand tapestry of existence.

CHAPTER - 3
THE MYTHOLOGY

CHAPTER - 3
THE MYTHOLOGY

Mythology, especially within Hinduism, is rich with stories that explain the origins of the universe, the nature of life, and the purpose of human existence. Central to Hindu mythology are the four Yugas and the ten avatars of Lord Vishnu, which serve as an allegory for cosmic cycles and divine intervention in times of chaos.

1. The Four Yugas

In Hindu cosmology, time is divided into four great eras known as Yugas. Each Yuga represents a stage of moral and spiritual decline or growth, and together they form one cycle known as a Mahayuga. These cycles repeat continuously, symbolizing the eternal nature of time.

1.1. Satya Yuga (Krita Yuga)

The Satya Yuga, or the Age of Truth, is the first and the most virtuous of the four Yugas. It is characterized by righteousness, virtue, and a close connection between humanity and the divine. In this era, people were highly spiritual, lived for thousands of years, and adhered strictly to the path of Dharma (moral values). There was no need for laws or punishments, as people naturally lived in harmony and truth.

1.2. Treta Yuga

The Treta Yuga, the second age, is marked by a decline in righteousness as humanity becomes more materialistic. Although Dharma is still present, it begins to diminish. In this Yuga, the great epic Ramayana is said to have taken place, featuring Lord Rama's quest to defeat the demon king Ravana. The Treta Yuga sees the emergence of divine heroes who guide humanity through the complexities of life.

1.3. Dvapara Yuga

The Dvapara Yuga is the third age, where
Dharma is further diminished, and human
behavior becomes more self-centered. This
period is known for the Mahabharata epic, where
the great battle of Kurukshetra took place. Lord
Krishna, one of the most revered incarnations of
Lord Vishnu, played a pivotal role as a guide and
divine strategist, imparting the teachings of the
Bhagavad Gita to Arjuna.

1.4. Kali Yuga

The Kali Yuga is the current age we are in,
marked by the greatest decline in righteousness.
This era is characterized by strife, deceit, and a
lack of spiritual knowledge. The average lifespan
of humans is shorter, and the focus shifts from
spiritual pursuits to material gains. The Kali Yuga
is said to last for 432,000 years, and we are
currently in the latter part of this Yuga. According
to Hindu beliefs, this age will eventually end in
destruction, paving the way for the next cycle of
Satya Yuga.

2. The Ten Avatars of Lord Vishnu (Dashavatara)

Lord Vishnu, the preserver of the universe, is believed to incarnate in various forms, known as avatars, to restore cosmic balance and protect Dharma. The ten avatars, collectively known as Dashavatara, represent the different forms Vishnu takes when divine intervention is needed. Each avatar symbolizes a different stage of evolution and adaptation to the needs of the time.

2.1. Matsya (The Fish)

The first avatar, Matsya, took the form of a fish. Vishnu assumed this form to save the ancient sage Manu and his sacred writings from a great deluge that threatened to destroy all life. Matsya guided Manu's boat to safety, ensuring the survival of civilization.

2.2. Kurma (The Tortoise)

In the form of a tortoise, Kurma supported Mount Mandara, which was used as a churning rod during the Samudra Manthan (churning of the ocean) to obtain the nectar of immortality, amrita. This avatar demonstrated Vishnu's role as a support for the cosmic balance and the unyielding foundation of the universe.

2.3. Varaha (The Boar)

Varaha, the boar, is one of the most powerful
avatars of Vishnu. He took this form to rescue the
Earth, personified as the goddess Bhudevi, from
the demon king Hiranyaksha. Varaha lifted the
Earth from the depths of the cosmic ocean,
signifying the protection and restoration of the
world.

2.4. Narasimha (The Man-Lion)

Narasimha, the man-lion, incarnated to protect his devotee, Prahlada, from his tyrannical father, King Hiranyakashipu. The king had been granted a boon that made him invincible to humans and animals, but Narasimha appeared as a half-man, half-lion, and defeated the king, demonstrating Vishnu's power to protect his devotees and uphold justice.

2.5. Vamana (The Dwarf)

Vamana, the dwarf, incarnated to subdue the
demon king Bali, who had gained control over the
universe. Vamana asked for three paces of land,
and when granted, he expanded to cover the
entire cosmos in three steps, pushing Bali to the
underworld and restoring cosmic order.

2.6. Parashurama (The Warrior with an Axe)

Parashurama was born to rid the world of corrupt Kshatriya rulers who misused their power. With his divine axe, he vanquished 21 generations of warriors, symbolizing the destruction of corruption and the re-establishment of order.

2.7. Rama (The Prince of Ayodhya)

Rama, the hero of the Ramayana, is one of the most beloved avatars of Vishnu. His story, characterized by virtue, sacrifice, and devotion, shows his journey from prince to king as he battled the demon king Ravana to rescue his wife, Sita. Rama exemplifies the ideals of dharma, loyalty, and righteousness.

2.8. Krishna (The Divine Lover and Philosopher)

Krishna, perhaps the most popular avatar, is the central figure of the Bhagavad Gita and the Mahabharata. He was a divine guide, friend, and lover, revealing deep spiritual truths and teachings that continue to resonate with people today. Krishna's life stories include his childhood exploits, his guidance to Arjuna on the battlefield, and his role in restoring justice and truth.

2.9. Buddha (The Enlightened One)

In some Hindu traditions, the ninth avatar of Vishnu is considered to be Siddhartha Gautama, known as Buddha. This avatar was believed to be an incarnation aimed at teaching compassion and renouncing the materialistic desires that had crept into society. Buddha's teachings emphasized the path of enlightenment and non-violence, resonating with humanity's need for peace and inner harmony.

2.10. Kalki (The Future Savior)

The tenth and final avatar, Kalki, is yet to appear. Kalki is predicted to arrive at the end of Kali Yuga, riding a white horse with a sword in hand to bring an end to the current age of darkness and to restore a new cycle of Satya Yuga. This avatar signifies the ultimate triumph of good over evil and the beginning of a new era of righteousness.

CHAPTER - 4

THE SCIENTIFIC EVIDENCE OF EVOLUTION AND SPIRITUAL PARALLELS

CHAPTER - 4

THE SCIENTIFIC EVIDENCE OF EVOLUTION AND SPIRITUAL PARALLELS

In this chapter, we will delve into the scientific evidence supporting evolution and draw parallels with the stories and teachings found in Hindu mythology. The theory of evolution, proposed by Charles Darwin, has changed the way we understand the development of life on Earth. From simple microorganisms in the primordial oceans to the complex life forms we see today, evolutionary biology has shown us that life is a continuous, gradual process shaped by natural selection and adaptation.

The fossil record, genetic evidence, and the study of embryology all support the idea that life evolved over millions of years. Fossils provide a historical record of organisms that lived in different eras, showing how life forms transitioned from simple to more complex structures. Genetic similarities between humans and other primates, as well as the presence of vestigial structures, point to a shared ancestry among species. Embryological evidence, which highlights the similarities in the early stages of development between different species, further reinforces the idea of a common origin.

Now, let's draw connections between this scientific understanding and the teachings found in Hindu mythology. The stages of evolution reflected in the story of the ten avatars of Lord Vishnu mirror the scientific progression of life. For instance, the first avatars, Matsya (the fish) and Kurma (the tortoise), represent the transition from aquatic life to semi-terrestrial existence. As evolution advanced, Varaha (the boar) symbolizes the rise of mammals from reptilian ancestors. The Vamana avatar, depicting the dwarf Brahmin, could signify early human forms that began to walk upright.

Parashurama, the warrior sage, represents a stage where humans developed tools and knowledge, which aligns with the emergence of Homo sapiens with increased cognitive abilities. Rama and Krishna symbolize the evolution of consciousness and intellect, depicting humans who understood complex concepts of morality, philosophy, and advanced societal structures. The avatars of Gautam Buddha and Kalki convey the ideals of spiritual perfection and the evolution of humanity to its highest potential.

By examining these parallels, we see that the narrative of Vishnu's avatars can be interpreted as a metaphor for the evolutionary journey of life, blending ancient teachings with modern scientific understanding. This integration reinforces the idea that spirituality and science can coexist and complement each other, offering a richer and more comprehensive understanding of our origins and existence.

CHAPTER - 5
BRIDGING EVOLUTION AND VISHNU'S AVATARS

CHAPTER - 5

BRIDGING EVOLUTION AND VISHNU'S AVATARS

To understand the interconnectedness between the scientific concept of evolution and the Hindu mythology of Vishnu's avatars, we need to view them through a lens that sees both as narratives of progress, adaptation, and the enduring quest for balance. Evolution explains the physical and biological development of life on Earth, while Vishnu's avatars symbolize spiritual and cosmic evolution, embodying the divine intervention required to maintain harmony. This chapter seeks to explore how these two perspectives—scientific and mythological—complement each other in the grand scheme of existence.

1. The Scientific Foundation of Evolution

The theory of evolution, as described by Charles Darwin, states that life originated in simple forms and gradually evolved into more complex beings through natural selection. Life began in the primordial waters, where microorganisms were the first signs of existence. Over time, these early life forms adapted to their environments, leading to the development of more complex organisms, eventually leading to the emergence of mammals, and then hominids. The story of human evolution, with our shared ancestry with apes, represents a long and transformative process—one that aligns with the idea of gradual progress.

2. The Avatars of Vishnu as a Symbolic Evolution

The concept of Vishnu's avatars can be seen as metaphors for stages of evolution, not just in a physical sense, but in a spiritual and moral context. Each avatar marks a period when divine intervention was required to bring balance and protect Dharma. The progression of these avatars can be paralleled with evolutionary stages, each incarnation responding to the needs of the time and representing a higher order of consciousness and existence.

2.1. Matsya (The Fish)

In the evolutionary timeline, the first life forms emerged in the water, which aligns with the story of Matsya, the fish. This avatar symbolizes the beginning of life in water and represents the transition from the most basic living beings to more complex organisms. Matsya's role in saving humanity during the great deluge signifies the importance of the aquatic phase as the cradle of life.

2.2. Kurma (The Tortoise)

Kurma, the tortoise, represents the next step in evolution—the transition from aquatic life to semi-aquatic and land-dwelling creatures. As reptiles, tortoises mark an evolutionary leap from fishes. The tortoise embodies adaptability and the gradual shift to life on land, indicating the development of complex life forms that could thrive in both water and on land. This phase of evolution set the foundation for further adaptations to terrestrial living.

2.3. Varaha (The Boar)

Varaha, the boar, signifies the further evolutionary leap from reptiles to mammals. The boar represents the emergence of mammals, creatures with more complex body structures and higher intelligence compared to reptiles. This stage embodies the development of warm-blooded beings capable of survival in varied environments. The boar's act of rescuing the Earth highlights the importance of mammals in maintaining ecological balance and the continuation of life on Earth.

2.4. Narasimha (The Man-Lion)

Narasimha, the man-lion, embodies the progression towards more intelligent and complex beings, bridging the gap between animal and human. This avatar symbolizes the development of hominids, early ancestors of modern humans who showed signs of intellect and emotional complexity. Narasimha's role in protecting Prahlada emphasizes the resilience of higher beings capable of overcoming existential challenges.

2.5. Vamana (The Dwarf)

The Vamana avatar represents the first recognizable human form in evolution. In the timeline of human development, this stage indicates the emergence of beings with human-like features and the potential for advanced thought and communication. The story of Vamana's request for three paces of land and his expansion to cover the universe symbolizes the transition from primitive beings to early humans who began to explore and claim their surroundings.

2.6. Parashurama (The Warrior with an Axe)

Parashurama's avatar signifies the early humans' advancement in tools and technology. The axe, a symbol of human ingenuity, marks the period when humans began to craft tools for hunting, building, and defense. Early humans used stone axes and other tools to hunt and survive, which laid the foundation for societal development. This stage represents the ingenuity and resourcefulness that propelled human progress.

2.7. Rama (The Prince of Ayodhya)

The incarnation of Rama represents the period when humans began to understand their surroundings and developed complex societies. Humans gained knowledge about governance, righteousness, and moral values. The epic of Rama's life highlights human potential for great deeds, exploration of human emotions, and the development of social order. This avatar signifies that humans reached an understanding of their purpose, society's values, and moral responsibility.

2.8. Krishna (The Divine Lover and Philosopher)

Krishna, the most revered of Vishnu's avatars, embodies the modern human. This stage represents the height of human intellect and technological innovation. Krishna's teachings in the Bhagavad Gita integrate knowledge, devotion, and action, signifying a phase when human beings have transcended mere survival and begun exploring advanced concepts of spirituality, technology, and the harmonious balance between the material and spiritual worlds. Krishna himself invented tools and innovations that demonstrated advanced human thought and capability, showcasing humanity's shift towards progress.

2.9. Buddha (The Enlightened One)

The Buddha avatar represents the emergence of the perfect human form, one who seeks inner peace, enlightenment, and wisdom. This stage in evolution signifies a shift from external achievements to an internal understanding of life. Siddhartha Gautama's teachings emphasize compassion, mindfulness, and liberation from material desires, marking the evolution of human consciousness towards enlightenment.

2.10. Kalki (The Future Savior)

Kalki represents the final stage of evolution as humanity enters a new cycle. This future avatar signifies the end of the current age of darkness, or Kali Yuga, and the beginning of a new era, Satya Yuga, where human beings will embody the highest form of virtue, wisdom, and understanding. Kalki's arrival symbolizes the transition from the current state of human development to an enlightened and advanced form, where the principles of balance, morality, and divine consciousness will prevail.

3. Bridging Evolution and Mythology

Both the theory of evolution and the story of Vishnu's avatars highlight adaptation, survival, and the pursuit of higher states of existence. While evolution explains the physical journey from single-celled organisms to humans and beyond, the avatars illustrate the moral and spiritual growth needed to reach higher levels of understanding and existence. Both concepts emphasize that life is a continuous journey of change, adaptation, and improvement, whether it be in the physical realm or the spiritual.

The avatars of Vishnu serve as metaphors for humanity's inherent potential to evolve not just biologically, but spiritually and morally. These stories teach that each stage of existence—be it the microscopic beginnings in the oceans or the more profound understandings of the divine—are interconnected. Life is an ongoing cycle of challenges, growth, and transcendence. Just as evolution continues to shape humanity, the avatars of Vishnu remind us that there will always be divine guidance to restore balance, inspire, and lead us to higher levels of existence.

CHAPTER - 6
KRISHNA VASUDEV

CHAPTER - 6
KRISHNA VASUDEV

In this final chapter, we explore the life and teachings of Lord Krishna, one of the most revered and enigmatic figures in Hindu mythology. Krishna Vasudev, as he is known, embodies the peak of human potential, showcasing not only divine power but also profound wisdom, love, and the understanding of life's ultimate purpose. His life story is not just a tale of divinity; it is a representation of humanity's deepest aspirations and the realization of our true nature.

1. The Birth and Early Life of Krishna

Krishna's story begins with his miraculous birth to Vasudev and Devaki in the prison of Kansa, the tyrannical ruler of Mathura. His life was marked by divine intervention from the start—escaping the clutches of death through divine will and being raised by his foster parents, Nanda and Yashoda, in the village of Gokul. This birth, under miraculous circumstances, symbolizes that even amidst darkness and oppression, light and hope can be born to lead and guide humanity.

2. Krishna as the Divine Teacher and Philosopher

Krishna's teachings in the Bhagavad Gita are among the most influential and timeless discourses on life, duty, and spirituality. Delivered to Arjuna on the battlefield of Kurukshetra, the Gita presents Krishna as the supreme guide who imparts profound wisdom that transcends time and culture. One of the most striking revelations Krishna shared was about the nature of human existence and the divine spirit that resides within all beings.

Krishna made a remarkable statement regarding the composition of the human body. He explained that every human or animal body is made up of the same elemental particles that make up the earth itself. This statement has a fascinating connection to modern scientific understandings.

The human body is composed of essential elements such as carbon, hydrogen, oxygen, nitrogen, phosphorus, and sulfur, which are also found in the composition of the earth. This concept aligns with the idea that humans are not separate from the earth but are inherently connected to it, an intricate part of its eternal cycle. The principle suggests that our physical existence is intrinsically tied to the elements of the natural world and theat we share the same origins.

Krishna's teachings also convey that the soul within each living being is eternal. While the physical body is temporary, the spirit, or Atman, moves on to a new form after the death of the physical body. This idea reflects the scientific principle of energy conservation, where energy, such as the soul, cannot be destroyed; it can only change forms. This fundamental truth reveals the continuity of existence beyond physical mortality, emphasizing the eternal journey of the soul.

3. The Spiritual Significance of Krishna's Philosophy

Krishna's teachings to Arjuna are not only about the composition of the body and the soul but also about how humans should live in harmony with their inner truth and the divine order. The concept of Dharma, or righteous duty, is central to Krishna's teachings. He urged Arjuna to rise above personal desires and act in accordance with divine will. This teaching encourages us to act selflessly, without attachment to the results of our actions, thus reaching a state of higher consciousness.

Krishna's words imply that the essence of being human is to recognize our divine connection to the cosmos. The Paramatma (the supreme spirit) within each of us is a fragment of the infinite, and understanding this truth can lead to spiritual awakening and liberation. He emphasized that true fulfillment comes from understanding one's connection to this higher consciousness and living a life of purpose, compassion, and wisdom.

4. The Legacy of Krishna's Teachings

Krishna Vasudev remains a beacon of how humans can embody divine qualities when they strive for truth, love, and wisdom. In this chapter, we have explored how Krishna not only represents the modern human but also serves as the ideal of progress that merges spirituality with earthly existence. His life is a testament to the idea that while humans evolve through different stages of physical and intellectual growth, the ultimate goal remains the same—to attain self-realization and spiritual fulfillment.

Krishna's life and teachings remind us that human beings are part of an eternal cycle, both physically and spiritually connected to the earth and the cosmos. His statement about the composition of the human body and the elements of the earth emphasizes the profound connection between humanity and the natural world. It serves as a powerful reminder that we are not separate from the earth; rather, we are an integral part of it, sharing the same fundamental elements that make up all life.

Krishna's teachings inspire us to see beyond the physical world, urging us to recognize the divine within ourselves and strive for a higher existence. They encourage us to understand that life is a continuous journey of growth, transformation, and discovery, ultimately leading to the realization of our true nature as part of the eternal spirit.

In essence, Krishna Vasudev is more than an incarnation; he is a symbol of the evolved human being who can navigate the complexities of life with grace, wisdom, and love. His life teaches us that evolution—whether seen through the lens of science or spirituality—is about reaching toward higher truths and living a life of integrity, love, and enlightenment. Krishna's legacy is a powerful reminder that the path of progress, both scientifically and spiritually, is a journey to understanding our true nature and realizing the divine within.

CONCLUSION
BRIDGING SCIENCE AND SPIRITUALITY

CONCLUSION
BRIDGING SCIENCE AND SPIRITUALITY

As we close the chapters of Genesis Redefined: Bridging Evolution and Divinity, we arrive at a deeper understanding of the interplay between science and spirituality. This book aimed to explore the origins of life from both a scientific and mythological perspective, demonstrating that these two realms—often considered separate—actually converge to reveal a more holistic view of existence.

The examination of Adam and Eve in the biblical narrative and the scientific story of evolution brought forth the realization that while religious teachings have deeply influenced human understanding of life's origins, modern science provides the empirical evidence to support and extend these beliefs. From the primordial soup to the first living cells in water, from the evolution of early hominids to the emergence of Homo sapiens, we see that life has followed a complex yet harmonious path, one that has echoes in the divine stories of Hindu mythology.

The narratives of the four Yugas and the ten avatars of Lord Vishnu show a progression, illustrating humanity's spiritual and physical evolution. The avatars, from Matsya the fish to Kalki the future warrior, map a timeline that parallels the stages of evolution. The tortoise, Kurma, suggests the transition from aquatic life to semi-terrestrial existence, while Varaha as the boar marks the evolutionary shift to mammalian life. The subsequent avatars, such as Vamana and Parashurama, reflect the evolution of human intelligence and the development of tools. Rama and Krishna highlight the advent of conscious, learned beings who grasp higher truths, including the understanding of technology, society, and spirituality. The teachings of Gautam Buddha and the representation of Kalki as the future figure further emphasize the evolution toward perfection and the ultimate potential of humanity.

Krishna's discourse in the Bhagavad Gita with Arjuna, especially his explanation that every human and animal body is made of the same elemental particles as the earth, merges scientific understanding with spiritual truth. This realization that the elements that constitute our physical bodies are the same as those found in the earth reinforces the notion that we are inherently part of the cosmos. Krishna's teachings remind us that life does not end with the death of the body; instead, the Atman (soul) transitions and continues its journey, signifying a fundamental cycle of existence, akin to the laws of energy conservation in science.

The conclusion of this book emphasizes that human evolution, whether approached through scientific theories or spiritual teachings, is a continuous journey of growth, change, and enlightenment. Our physical forms are intricate compositions of nature's elements, yet within us resides an eternal spirit. This recognition challenges us to see beyond the boundaries of our physical existence and to embrace a unified understanding of life, which merges scientific insight and spiritual wisdom. In this way, we can strive for a future where the search for knowledge is not just limited to what we can measure or observe but extends to an understanding of our profound connection to the universe, each other, and the eternal source from which all life originates.

Genesis Redefined ultimately invites us to look within and see the reflection of the cosmos in ourselves. It is a call to embrace our evolution, not just in the physical realm, but in the spiritual and intellectual dimensions as well, as we continue to seek deeper truths about our origins and purpose in this vast universe.

FINAL WORDS FROM THE AUTHOR

As we close this journey through the realms of science and spirituality, I hope this book has sparked new insights and opened doors to deeper understanding. It is my belief that the universe, with its infinite complexities, holds the answers to the questions that have fascinated humanity for millennia. Whether we seek knowledge through the lens of science or the wisdom of ancient philosophies, both paths ultimately lead to the same truth.

Thank you for taking the time to explore this intersection of evolution and divinity. I invite you to continue questioning, learning, and growing—because in the pursuit of knowledge, there is no end, only more profound beginnings.

I look forward to hearing your thoughts and continuing this dialogue with you.

With gratitude and curiosity,

Rameshwar Raj
Founder, RAM & CO

THANK YOU

www.ingramcontent.com/pod-product-compliance
Lightning Source LLC
Chambersburg PA
CBHW041651150726
48005CB00013BA/1615